GAZING

THROUGH

THE PRISM

OF LIFE

SANDRA GLASSMAN

Brilliant Books Literary
137 Forest Park Lane Thomasville
North Carolina 27360 USA

CONTENTS

A Day In The Life Of..1

An Evening Of Speed Dating 2

A Four Letter Word..3

As The Whistle Blows 4

Beautiful Sky..5

Cages 6

Communication..7

Craze For Eternal Youth 8

Dialogue Of Music..9

Don't Pull The Trigger..10

Dream Weaver..11

Eyes..12

Five Fingers 13

Food Sparks Passion 14

Giving Up 15

Guns And Society 16

Heart..18

If Only 19

It's Necessary To Wise Up..20

It's Only A Moment 21

Keys 22

Latte's And Chemistry..23

Love What Is It? 24

Menu For Life 25

Night Fright..26

Old Ball Game 27

On The Shelf 28

Paint... 29

Penny For Thoughts 30

Pillow Chatter 31

Planting A Thought 32

Poetry Is 33

Robbery 34

Sayings 35

Spinning... 36

Spiral Staircase.. 37

Sports Fans 38

Strategy 39

Summer-2003 40

Treasures 41

The Harp.. 42

Time Warp 43

To Each His Own 44

There Is No Point.. 45

To Say Or Not To Say 46

Unanswered Questions.. 47

Untitled.. 48

Walking Dead 49

Why I Write... 50

Word Rhyming 51

Worth Waiting For... 52

A DAY IN THE LIFE OF

Intimidated
Situated
Medicated
Liquidated
Saturated
Educated
Calculated
Incorporated
Agitated
An equal opportunity work day soliloquy

AN EVENING OF SPEED DATING

Enter into a huge gathering room
Each of us with an agenda
Awkward while hoping to appear sophisticated
Wondering if our attire is current or outdated
Whole truths may lead to unwanted conclusions
Too much voice, limited choice
Can sink a future relationship
Given a glimpse into someone's persona
Might deceive rather than relieve
Switching people, in the blink of an eye, makes
Gathering information difficult for future hookups
Judging on intuition my comment would be
Tiring for the brain, ending with repetitive refrain

A FOUR LETTER WORD

Safe a four letter word
Does everyone want to play it safe?
As enclosed in the cocoon of life
Guarded by invisible security blankets
Decisions played for safety versus risks
Potential hidden mind devours lost chances
Recriminations everblown to excess
Lapse time extremely short for indulging
In self pity
Safe, taken care of, protected, snug, unhappy!!!

AS THE WHISTLE BLOWS

The loud shrill note, of the tiny plastic device is a signal to
Pay attention, be alert, listen
When you're enjoying the day at the shore, and you hear that
Distinct sound, it signals someone is in need of aid or Assistance
Coaches, teachers, instructors, all use this tiny but effective
Tool to get attention
When a person is described as a whistle blower, they have
Information, that could be of vital importance
To industry or government, corporations
Don't ignore the tiny whistle
It's like a "S.O.S." for Batman
Pay attention just pucker up and blow

BEAUTIFUL SKY

Holiday fireworks light up the ebony
Sky, adding adornments to the heavens
Along with booming noises from bright rockets
Augment sound and music to the celebration
The chorus of stars, are sensitive to
An interruption of tranquility
Festivities offer fun to some
Those residing with a higher being
Do their best to accept

CAGES

Faces grimacing, mocking, staring
We look in, they are spellbound by
Intense curiosity, we gaze at the
Amusement mixed with glee
Quiz in motion with body language
Emotional ballet from sullen to animation
We, as humans' visit hoping to be provided
Entertainment, children throw food
At the cages laughing,
Anxiously clowning with gusto are the animals

Do we realize that they possess powerful
Maternal instincts as do we?
Can our supposedly superior brains
Learn anything from different species
A snap from a camera can capture
Expression from love to sadness and anger
On the animals in their caged lairs
Can society be sure that those caged
Are more inhuman or dangerous to the
Future of existence

COMMUNICATION

Tweeting tales of mean
Do reflect jealous envy of green
Tweeting is so baseless, as bowing to the English queen
Tales of banter the likes of which have never been seen
What does all this have to do with anything
The world still exists, don't pick the losers team

CRAZE FOR ETERNAL YOUTH

Motives given, better self-esteem if
Covered with advertised potion cream
Being sports active, socially mucho attractive
Less excess weight starts a clean slate

Means and ways to a happier you?
Botex injections-diminished rejection
Lipo- suck it up
Fill the vanity trophy cup
Before chest implants droopy
Magically transformed into a young groupie
Non kissable lips- painted finger tips
Flabby arms, lack of charms
Erase listless eyes- no cellulite thighs
***Beauty can't assure happiness
It must coexist with courage
Compassion towards humanity
Remember under the skin we are one

DIALOGUE OF MUSIC

Vivid hues awaken the brain
Vertical strokes accent the artist's clarity for detail
Tangible tranquility
Scenes and images display visual poetry hidden within
Musical notes and lyrical quotes abound
Endless discussion possibilities
Positive eye candy mobility
Interpretation open
Dialogue of music

DON'T PULL THE TRIGGER

LAND OF THE FREE, HOME OF THE BRAVE

Not so much anymore, hand guns, assault rifles,
Shot guns, pistols, make us vulnerable to
Look over our shoulder, while going about
Daily life
How can humans deal with the stresses?
Of guns in the hands of the mentally ill
People it seems are able to connive
Their way with money or drugs to
Seduce
For money people do stupid stuff,
Ignoring a logical thought
Fascination with violent video games
Action movies, killing innocent
Animals for fun
The written word is sometimes
"THE BEST WEAPON"

DREAM WEAVER

While in a pre-somnolent state, as frequently occurs
Trying valiantly to distress from the day's events
My bed looks so inviting, I actually hear it summon
Me to lie down, wanting to oblige totally, although
My active and awake brain decides to spin round
And round like a roulette wheel spitting out words
Thoughts, ideas hovering over my tired body
All I desire is sleep but if I don't have my pad
And pencil at the night table the great poems
Will vanish-erased by the time daylight presents
I will have lost my beautiful poetry.

EYES

The eyes support her
The eyes dry now, but still so black
Looking like shining lumps of coal
Eyes so puffy from tears and enormous
Challenges of her life's turbulent past
Her eyes tell a story, wide with joy
Eyes glowing from the embers of a forever love
Eyes searching for reasons and answers
Eyes gaining strength and purpose, one can see
Into her soul, in the beauty of them
The twilight years' approach views may dim
Never again as once they were
Truth of the eyes may be doubted

FIVE FINGERS

Five fingers on each hand
Enough for certain chores
Five fingers on each hand
Plenty of energy to seed or plow the land
Ten fingers likely to build
Castles in the sand
One can model shiny polished
Nails on a sun burnt wedding band
Fingers heal, hands and fingers
Work gently soothing to the
Touch, fingers create-magic
Accomplished, fingers work
Computers, iPads, tools
Hands alert taxi's
Babies are able to find their
Thumbs for contentment, where
Pulling the trigger finger can
Mean the end of innocent life
At stressful times one can lift
Up fingers towards the heavens
Above and praise the higher being

FOOD SPARKS PASSION

You're the chocolate covered strawberries of my passion
At times you bring out a taste of bitter lemons, so my
Eyes start to water
My smile emerges as the fragrance of salty French fries
Perks under my nostrils
Iced rainbow sherbet tickles my taste buds
As you lean over to kiss me, I await the nest course

GIVING UP

I've folded my tent
Wish I were able to locate a phone booth
And change my identity like Clark Kent
I can't accept the heart damage dent
I know you meant
So I must fold my tent

I refuse to wallow in self pity
Responsibilities and sanity force
Me to vent
You promised to pay the rent
Creditors are banging on my door
To bankrupt my every cent
All the affection and future up and went
I've folded my tent

GUNS AND SOCIETY

I shot you, you're dead! Joey and
I are playing in front of our house outside.
I tell Joey, I pulled my gun trigger first, so your dead.
Okay Joey says we should both pretend to fall down.
We are two six-year-old kids
playing cops and robbers or Cowboys and Indians.
Back in the 1950's a toy gun was always a boys play thing.
It was popular and one could improvise
like the shows on television.
The good cowboy or the sheriff wore a shiny silver star,
standing out on his jacket or shirt.
Around his hip were two holsters with guns.
The good guys shot the bad hombres and all was well.
When playing war games guns were the integral ingredient
Fast forward to the present.
Guns have become a disease,
A way around anger, revenge, mental illness.
Having a gun whether purchased legally or
on the street, assures the owner POWER!!!, unlimited POWER!
People do use guns for hunting deer, bears,
Lions, elephants for their ivory tusks, etc.
Guns kill animals and people.
Innocent children are no longer safe
from the whim of someone who has an agenda.
I can understand the argument of society
to own a firearm to protect their loved ones.
Ironically my friend Joey, that was my playmate
so many years ago, was fatally shot by a stray bullet,
meant for another, I am shattered.

Just an afterthought
Guns kill and ruin lives
Life is a precious gift
Each day through the hourglass
The sand does sift
Don't be a lone ship adrift
On the seas of apathy

HEART

You can't mend a broken heart with a needle
You can't stop a heart from beating by crying
You can cause a heart to feel chopped
Into pieces
The heart is a precise and sensitive
Instrument, like a violin
Treat your heart with velvet gloves
A heart can cease to beat over sadness
A bullet can!!! stop a heart

IF ONLY

We all have the desire for "the good life"
We desire things, we think are necessary
We complain, "if only I had more money
"If only I could be thinner"
If I had long beautiful hair
"If only" during my vacation to another
Country I found a painting, worth thousands
Of dollars, and I paid twenty dollars would
I suddenly acquire happiness?
"If only" I married a man that held me
In his heart, instead of beating me on a Daily basis
How many times while viewing magazines that
Feature outlandish, over the top homes and
Dream "Wow" if only I could afford such
Luxury
Good fortune and everlasting joy, may seem
Inviting, but life is so breakable
Nobody escapes, there is always twists and turns,
What can be the explanation?
For cruelty, to other humans suffering
Terminal illness, severe disabilities, finding
Joy in peoples' woes
Some of society are able to accept the "cards
They were dealt" Perhaps faith plays a large
Role in one's character and ability to offer
A genuine helping hand, be in harmony, with
Our fellow humans

IT'S NECESSARY TO WISE UP

What's up with so many untruths
The headlines scream "scandals"
Newspapers and news TV. Salivate for
More, never enough we start our day on technical devices
To become taken hostage to other peoples opinions
Talking heads for the government
Journalists parroting and reporting
Sent from higher ups to get the scoops
Some say white lies are necessary to
Achieve certain goals
Keeping the public in the dark
Don't rock the boat snooping by
The IRS the false reporting on Bengazi
Edward Snowden? Hero or villain
Take your pick
We the voters elect on promises
So false why are we so easily duped
Society should wise up
The proof isn't on the book jacket
Perhaps the answer is not money spent
We deserve to have our elected
Officials serve us

IT'S ONLY A MOMENT

It's only a moment, my eyes glisten with
Delight at the thought of savoring the
Shiny chocolate morsel on the kitchen
Table within my grasp

Residing there testing my discipline
And will power, temptation has eluded
Me so far, my finger sticks say sugar
Under control
I chew over (so to speak) the situation
Finally, I succumb, it's only a moment
The devil made me do it!!!!!

KEYS

Private keys to the heart
For the one you love
Keys to a car
Key to the city
Key to unlock a mystery
Key for house
Key for hotel mini bar
Keys to the kingdom
Keys on a piano
Key for a storage locker
Safety deposit box key
Key for gym lock

K-IS FOR KEEPING
E-IS FOR ENTRY
Y-IS TRULY YOURS
S-STOLEN RESULT HEADACHE!!!

LATTE'S AND CHEMISTRY

The anticipation to hook up
Tried numerous Internet sites
Promises of a connection to love
NO guarantees, no clues with hand held techno device
To seal the deal
Single Mingle, EHarmony, Match.com etc,
which to choose?
Finally, I agree to meet for a Latte
At a fashionable bistro
First rule, sit near window for a close-up
To view and get strong or weak vibe
Mind spinning thoughts, question to stay or leave?
Should I take the chance?
will this be another dead end?

LOVE WHAT IS IT?

What is this thing called love? it's just a four
Letter word, mysterious, emotional, harsh, often
Misunderstood. Since the beginning of recorded time
Humans as well as the animal kingdom acted out their
Depiction of what we think of as love with gestures
Or verbal sounds. Today in the year 2015, everybody
Uses this word through their media devices, written
Letters, sign language, we rely on our smart phones.
At work one may receive a text message to break up
A love relationship, without so much as a caring
Thought to the person who is the recipient.
Presently, we use the word love for practically
Everything we do. we love our pets, God, food, special
Events, entertainment, our family and children
This word love, which has sentimental meaning to most
Slips off our tongues as if waterfall without ending
Society loves to exaggerate the meaning of the love with
verbal nonsense, one can't love absolutely everything
Some of the population uses the word to imply harm or
Hatred, such as "I would love to beat that person to a
Pulp!" what's up with that, we come into this world like
A blank piece of paper. Yet in the present, there are wars
And conflicts everywhere. Where is the "Love".
As I write this small article, I'm blown away by the
inconsistent rhetoric we accept today

MENU FOR LIFE

At times life is like a meal
You first approach it with hunger and zeal
Maybe the menu leaves a lot to be desired
So proceed with caution, until you feel inspired
Take a chance the menu is abundant
Being unable to choose would be redundant
As time passes your hunger may diminish
So you settle for the hum-drum
To finally finish
Life offers a very full plate, so don't nibble
Take a big bite, and soon you'll see
Just how big your appetite can be

NIGHT FRIGHT

Closed and mysterious in the dark of night
Curiosity peeked by flickerin candle light
Shadowy glow illuminates museum treasures
At daylight public strolls through
While at their leisure
Light out at night, suddenly a moan, a growl
A blood curling groan
Perchance a dropped dinosaur bone?
Who goes there? An intruder
All who reside inside react with alarm
Will the museum animals suffer any harm?
Quizative glances dart back and forth
Does the intruder wish a fight?
Don't mess with creatures they can bite
A few moments elapse-not to worry
Situation resolved in a hurry
The interruption problem taken care
Only a clumsy ghost slithering through there

OLD BALL GAME

Let's go to the old ball game
When millions of dollars weren't
The only aim
Hero's came to bat without shame
And stolen bases, bunts, home runs
Weren't stunts for strutting fame
Today's baseball is tainted by hints
That the guys are pumped up before
The season starts
Old fans boarded the subways and came
To see their favorites, play with passion
New records are set every day steroids rule
And are to be blame
Shame on artificial substances for lowering
Standards for this and other sports
Take me out to the "OLD BALL GAME'

ON THE SHELF

I haven't been able to open this door
For twelve months, three days, four hours
My daughter's favorite possessions are
Subtle reminders, Today I must enter

Somehow I summon up courage
Tears are long dismissed from my eyes
My insides are shriveled, slowly I pry
The door slightly ajar peeking inside
The handmade shelf, the one she helped
To make, she adorned it with her special
Memories, awards, trophies, some junk

Tessa's most shabby but loveable stuffed
Bear sits, his button eyes are sad
As if waiting for her return
My eyes dart back and forth, to much sadness
Reality hits me in the pit of my stomach
I realize the healing time is not yet over

PAINT

Jackson Pollack famous artist
Paintings are dramatic, passionate, vivid
Mish mosh of colors and striking movements
If canvas were a globe his artistic renderings
Could capture the tumultuous recent events
In a realistic scene of carnage, floods, earthquakes
Wars, fires, nature's fury
His interpretation would look like a frenzy of action
Very sadly this is reality

PENNY FOR THOUGHTS

Where are You, when the plane was blown
Out of the beautiful blue sky
Where are YOU, hearing about innocent people
Whose blood is being the décor of the streets
Where are you when a young policeman was
The target for a deranged killer without mercy
Perhaps I should ask "Where is your voice"
I know silence is not heard, outrage is loud
The scope of humanity, such as it is must
React, why it refuses remains a mystery

PILLOW CHATTER

Whether you lay your head on down, goose feathers
Foam rubber, silk, cotton, or the most expensive of
Materials, the resulting slumber may be hazardous
To your life and limb
Some say talk is cheap
On a pillow, talk may be quite deep
Secrets, lies, videotape,
Betrayal, cheating, clandestine meetings
Stock tips given away, markets downward spiral
If humans weren't swayed by romance
To spill all, not take the chance
Can pillow chatter turn chaotic?
Sealed lips may make the difference
Between disaster and victory

PLANTING A THOUGHT

Under an umbrella of floral,
The blanket of nature takes form
Glory is the culmination of planted ideology
There can be no victories with collateral damages
Fists as weapons, verbal tools as sanity
Can you feel my pain?
Can I express feelings for yours?
How's that working for us
Get a grip on the pulse of humanity

POETRY IS

Poetry Is, Popping open a can of alphabet soup
Place into microwave, heat and serve
Viola !!!Liquid poetry in motion

Poetry Is, A potpourri of life's ups and downs
Poetry Is, words and music
Poetry Is, Fodder for a sleepless night

ROBBERY

It creeps, it crawls, advances fast, sometimes stalls
It's not a robber with a mask, no shootum up bang-bang
Too much attention needed to be a bore
Too much urgency for a cure
Robbery of one's mind, robbery of dignity
Victim and family no longer in control
Heart wrenching choices, placement in unfamiliar territory
Journey of futility, victim lost forever

SAYINGS

The beauty of symmetry can be seen by the mind
Even in poverty, pride and courage can shine
Isolation doesn't mean deprivation
The ultimate plateau is not always height It's knowledge
The earth spins the mind's camera snaps pictures
The eye helps to see what the mind already knows
Laughter is the key, life is the door

SPINNING

These current times are spinning out of control
Can tell you so, no other words will suffice
Nobody loves their neighbor
NO one gives a higher being its due
Trouble lurking all around us, be vigilant
Chaos and disarray, if we ignore the golden rule
Some flourish with taking risks, pleasure seekers
Choosing the path to destruction comes easy
Inequality, poverty, lack of employment, fosters
Deep resentment, anger festers and boils over"
Have and Have Nots" will always be
At times, solutions to difficult questions
Are elusive

SPIRAL STAIRCASE

Seen frequently in the flicks of long ago
Was the spiral staircase
It became a fixture in the movie plot,
As a vehicle for murder and mystery
Accidents galore with gore
The villain usually shoved, pushed, tripped
Or was shot
Hollywood loved the actor or actress falling
On cue
Spike heels would catch, arguments would be
Settled the spiral staircase was a popular
With the director, for visual effects as
Were cars stranded on train tracks
Presently movies have amped up the
Special sights and sounds, and technology
And blood spilling out all around
That being said, the now can't recapture
What was the intrigue and thrill of
Holding one's breath as someone was
Falling down the spiral staircase

SPORTS FANS

Crowds flock, beer floats, rowdy banter
Sportswriters take notes, losing team gets the boos
Top pitcher balks, hasn't a clue
Out of the dugout the manager appears with a scowl
Angry fans hoot and howl
If the home team happens to lose, fans will yell fowl
Another sports event with drunks, fights, and sunburn
Sit back and enjoy the expenses for a crummy day

STRATEGY

Ever order from a restaurant menu?
So many choices, so many voices
Different combinations weight gaining hesitations
The same strategy can apply to business
Divide responsibilities for the appetizer
Hire qualified personal for the main course
Keep abreast from the smallest, to the largest detail
React to change when situations arise
The right choices from business menu's
Can mean the difference between an intelligent
selection and avoiding indigestion
To sum up! Don't surmise be ready to compromise
For no pain –Hopefully only financial gain

SUMMER-2003

Pale white sea gulls munching on anything
Ten a.m. Sunny, summer morn
Still visible. Previous days rubbish
The wire pails filled with trash remains uncollected
Surfers in latex garb atop their boards
Awaiting the next giant wave
The beige shiny sand not yet cluttered
By multicolored beach chairs, umbrella's
Pails and shovels, food aroma's
At the sands edge, water gently flows to and fro
Rippling to a slow dance rhythm
Luminating under the water, sea shells
Treasure for children to discover
Overhead, a large gray cloud appears
Looming above this tranquil scene
Out of the slight haze a deafening flourish
Of trumpet noise
Lifeguards perched atop the sand, ready to
Start the day, cover with a hand their eyes
To see an unbelievable image for the mind
Aircraft slowly approaching releasing
From the aircraft underbelly numerous parachutes
The aura of relaxation fades, what is the interruption
Perhaps preparation for a terrorist attack.
Suddenly a day at the beach now includes
Fun tempered with extreme caution

TREASURES

Treasure what can it be?
The sight and odor of a fresh cut pine tree
Are glittering rubies and diamonds or green wads
Of paper bills all that you see?
A human being may be one in a million possessing
Extraordinary qualities that long endure
Treasure the ebb and flow of white capped waves
So majestic as they wend their way to the shore
Counting gold dabloons and pieces of eight are
Never a bore
The power of spiritual belief offers a treasure
Worth so much more
Greed and lust turn some in society to fight a war
Treasure can be a love song, a child's gentle touch
Fresh lilacs, a compliment, a group of birds as they soar
To each his own every day is too precious to ignore
Treasure what you have for that might be the big score

THE HARP

Pluck the strings with daintiest of fingers
Careful not to injure fleshy digits
Stately instrument immensely hard to manage
Results beautiful serene music
Pleasure by a lit fireplace in winter

TIME WARP

I hope my imagination isn't racing overtime
Everything's upside down
People are going through their daily life's
Eyes starring with complete emptiness
No happy visions apparent in their gazes
No direction, no people connection
Society totally absorbed with technical
Advances, such a waste of time
World spinning, changing with every heart
Beat, I'm in a time warp
Looking back to the past in retrospect
I should have appreciated calmer times
Grabbed at given opportunities
Nothing could have prepared me for
This time warp mentality
A full dose of reality
Moral and social banality
Is this time warp finality?

TO EACH HIS OWN

Shelter and comfort have different meanings
Each member of society deals with their journey
Through life's twists and turns as well as they can
There is no invisible umbrella, life is life
Some find comfort reciting a poignant prayer
Others succumb to bubbly beer
Perhaps pills can make us care
A braggart's dare lucky coin so rare
Romance to share
Hiding in a grizzly's empty lair
Whatever helps to get you there

THERE IS NO POINT

Look at a flower! all beautiful and limbed
Petals stately, perfumed and trimmed
Does it matter if their straight or gay?
Can it have a message to display?
There is so much attention to societies
Baseless, factless anti-gay sentiment
Mob mentality's rush to judgement
Social and mental differences shouldn't
Be a catalyst for subhuman actions
Teens and younger children are in a
State of flux, people who gossip are
Bullies, electronic means of communication
Contribute spreading rumor and intolerance
"RAINBOWS ARE DIFFERENT"
To harm is a crime don't do the deed
What's the point! there isn't reason or rhyme

TO SAY OR NOT TO SAY

Tell me I'm smart, tell me I'm lazy
Don't say I'm beautiful, that makes me crazy
Words are cheap, words are incomplete
Smooth talking words can cause one to weep
The wrong words can spark a suicide leap
Don't fill my head with complements
They don't hit the mark, don't say I'm beautiful
Looks are deceiving, there's so much more to me
Don't try to contact me, I'm leaving

UNANSWERED QUESTIONS

The falling leaves liberate the tree's
Shedding their summer attire to welcome
The change to another season, so many
Tree's perish from the wrath of nature
Curbside one can view the damage first hand
Squirrels scamper with nourishment to prepare
For winter
Do the tree's feel lighter and therefore miss the
Attention from passing cars viewing the glorious
Color changes as fall approaches?
Are the downed and sick tree's part of a community
That equates loss as humans do?
Do they have a sense of sadness?
No answer to this question.

UNTITLED

Wipe the slate clean?
What does that really mean?
Blackboard, eraser, click of the mouse?
Quick fix, change of venue, slight of hand
Written words can be so powerful, think
Harm from bullet
Changing requires pain and goals
A spotless mind is unattainable
Memories remain

WALKING DEAD

Fire up the TV on any day
Low and behold a multitude of zombies
Fill up the screen
Walking dead doing zombie stroll
Reality!! what's up with that
Entertainment glorifying these actions
Flesh, gore, and dripping blood
Is there anything more riveting?
Society hung up on this latest craze
Zombies don't wear snazzy attire
The goal of the walking dead is
Their obsession to target revenge
And proclaim victory with a pound
Of Live flesh
Come on. now!! this really feeding
Our pleasure appetite

WHY I WRITE

The mime does his elaborate hand and
Body gestures
To display the thoughts and feelings
The artist with palate and brush and
Specific images, conveys his ideas
Through color and brings to life
His essay on canvas to completion
The poet with accompanying parts of
Speech, serves up turmoil, affection,
Illness, religion, emotions, stories
And thus can entertain and educate
Preferring to remain voiceless
But expressive
The mime playfully demonstrates
Sound is not necessary

WORD RHYMING

Can't eat a lemon without scrunching up your face
Comfortable camping will not be a pleasure
Absent a good space
Enhance the chance at the casino by
Pokering an ace
Purchase the most expensive set of wheels
To win the race
Baseball players must run around the diamond to
Slide into home base
Women could feel safer by packing mace
Sexy clothes trimmed with ribbons and lace
We hope our tax refunds are returned in a swift pace
Rhyming can be fun, you will have a smiley face

WORTH WAITING FOR

I read the ad imagined my name in lights
I got to have the courage to be the best
If I fail others will pass the test
I could be great, I might be bad
I audition for the role, hoping to reach
My goal
To much stress causes my heart to pound
Got to keep the focus
I'm Broadway bound
I'll cross my fingers
I've made it to the final round
Have to memorize the script
To be able to understudy other parts
It's opening night my knees are shaking
The heavy makeup on my face under the lights
Could smudge and smear
But I'm on the Broadway stage
I don't care
Curtain comes down to loud applause
My family is proud the roar of the crowd
Continues the cast bows
This night can't be replaced
I've finally made it, my name is in playbill

www.ingramcontent.com/pod-product-compliance
Lightning Source LLC
Chambersburg PA
CBHW020343130626

46549CB00003B/1270